Garfield

On Top Of The World

JIM DAVIS

RAVETTE BOOKS

First published by Ravette Books Limited 1989
Reprinted 1990, 1991 (twice), 1993

Printed and bound in Great Britain
for Ravette Books Limited,
8 Clifford Street,
London W1X 1RB
An Egmont Company
by Cox & Wyman Ltd, Reading

ISBN 1 85304 104 1

© 1987 United Feature Syndicate, Inc.

© 1987 United Feature Syndicate, Inc.

JIM DAVIS 11-25

I'M SORRY GARFIELD. I DIDN'T SEE YOU SITTING ...

THERE

JIM DAVIS 11-26

JiM DAViS 11-27

NOW, **THAT'S** GOOD COFFEE!

JIM DAVIS 12-1

© 1987 United Feature Syndicate, Inc.

© 1987 United Feature Syndicate, Inc.

© 1987 United Feature Syndicate, Inc.

OH, NO! WHAT HAPPENED TO MY TOES?!

© 1987 United Feature Syndicate, Inc.

JIM DAVIS   1-1-88

© 1987 United Feature Syndicate, Inc.

PSSSSSH

THIS STUFF IS GUARANTEED TO KEEP PETS OFF THE FURNITURE

© 1987 United Feature Syndicate, Inc.

IT'S SO EASY IT'S ALMOST UNFAIR

JIM DAVIS

1-9-88

© 1988 United Feature Syndicate, Inc.

© 1988 United Feature Syndicate, Inc.

© 1988 United Feature Syndicate, Inc.

© 1988 United Feature Syndicate, Inc.

JIM DAVIS 2-9

© 1988 United Feature Syndicate, inc.

GARFIELD, I HOPE YOU'RE NOT THINKING OF CLIMBING MY CURTAINS

I WOULDN'T DREAM OF CLIMBING YOUR STUPID CURTAINS, JON

© 1988 United Feature Syndicate, Inc.

BUT, TO BE THE FIRST CAT EVER TO LEAD AN EXPEDITION UP THE SOUTHWEST FACE OF MT. EVEREST, THAT'S ANOTHER MATTER!

JIM DAVIS

2-25

THEY SAY, "YOU ARE WHAT YOU EAT"

© 1988 United Feature Syndicate, Inc.

JIM DAVIS

3-8

MOOOO

© 1988 United Feature Syndicate, Inc.

© 1988 United Feature Syndicate, Inc.

© 1988 United Feature Syndicate, Inc.

OTHER GARFIELD BOOKS IN THIS SERIES

No. 1	Garfield The Great Lover	£2.50
No. 2	Garfield Why Do You Hate Mondays?	£2.50
No. 3	Garfield Does Pooky Need You?	£2.50
No. 4	Garfield Admit It, Odie's OK!	£2.50
No. 5	Garfield Two's Company	£2.50
No. 6	Garfield What's Cooking?	£2.50
No. 7	Garfield Who's Talking?	£2.50
No. 8	Garfield Strikes Again	£2.50
No. 9	Garfield Here's Looking At You	£2.50
No. 10	Garfield We Love You Too	£2.50
No. 11	Garfield Here We Go Again	£2.50
No. 12	Garfield Life and Lasagne	£2.50
No. 13	Garfield In The Pink	£2.50
No. 14	Garfield Just Good Friends	£2.50
No. 15	Garfield Plays It Again	£2.50
No. 16	Garfield Flying High	£2.50
No. 18	Garfield Happy Landings	£2.50
No. 19	Garfield Going Places	£2.50
No. 20	Garfield Le Magnifique!	£2.50
No. 21	Garfield In The Fast Lane	£2.50
No. 22	Garfield In Tune	£2.50
No. 23	Garfield The Reluctant Romeo	£2.50
No. 24	Garfield With Love From Me To You	£2.50
No. 25	Garfield A Gift For You	£2.50
No. 26	Garfield Great Impressions	£2.50

GARFIELD GALLERIES

Garfield Gallery No. 1	£4.95
Garfield Gallery No. 2	£4.95
Garfield Gallery No. 3	£4.95
Garfield Gallery No. 4	£4.95
Garfield Gallery No. 5	£4.95
Garfield Gallery No. 6	£4.95
Garfield Gallery No. 7	£4.95

GARFIELD COMIC ALBUMS

No. 1	Sitting Pretty	£3.99
No. 2	Words Of Wisdom	£3.99

COLOUR TV SPECIALS

Here Comes Garfield	£2.95
Garfield On The Town	£2.95
Garfield In The Rough	£2.95
Garfield In Disguise	£2.95
Garfield In Paradise	£2.95
Garfield Goes To Hollywood	£2.95
A Garfield Christmas	£2.95
Garfield's Thanksgiving	£2.95
Garfield's Feline Fantasies	£2.95
Garfield Gets A Life	£2.95
Garfield's Night Before Christmas	£3.95
Garfield's Tales Of Mystery	£3.95
Garfield's Scary Tales	£3.95
Garfield The Easter Bunny?	£3.95
Garfield Best Ever	£4.95
Garfield Selection	£5.95
Garfield His 9 Lives	£5.95
Garfield Diet Book	£4.95
Garfield Exercise Book	£4.95
Garfield Book Of Love	£2.99

All these books are available at your local bookshop or newsagent, or can be ordered direct from the publisher. Just tick the titles you require and fill in the form below. Prices and availability subject to change without notice.

Ravette Books, PO Box 11, Falmouth, Cornwall, TR10 9EN.

Please send a cheque or postal order for the value of the book, and add the following for postage and packing:
UK including BFPO – £1.00 per order.
OVERSEAS, including EIRE – £2.00 per order.
OR Please debit this amount from my Access/Visa Card (delete as appropriate).

Card Number ☐☐☐☐☐☐☐☐☐☐☐☐☐☐☐☐☐☐

AMOUNT £ ....   EXPIRY DATE ....

SIGNED ....

NAME ....

ADDRESS ....

....